# We Are Complete In Him

### An in-depth exposition of Colossians 2:10

## Lydia Olorunniwo

SOPHOS BOOKS

**We Are Complete In Him**
Copyright © 2025 by Lydia Olorunniwo

**Published by**
Sophos Books
Croydon
CR0 0AZ
*sophosbooks.com*

Unless otherwise stated, all scriptures quotations are taken from The Holy Bible, *New King James Version* of the Bible, Copyright © 1982 Thomas Nelson.

All rights reserved. No part of this publication may be reproduced, stored in a retrieval system, or transmitted in any form or by any means, mechanical, electronic photocopying or otherwise without prior written consent of the copyright owner.

ISBN 978-1-905669-46-2

Cover design by Tope Enoch.
Printed in the United Kingdom.

# Contents

| | |
|---|---|
| Dedication | V |
| Acknowledgements | VII |
| Author's Preface | IX |
| Foreword | XI |
| Introduction | 1 |
| 1. Understanding Completeness | 9 |
| 2. The Deity of Christ | 19 |
| 3. Our Identity in Christ | 25 |
| 4. When Strength Fails, Grace Prevails | 31 |
| 5. The Power of the Cross | 37 |
| 6. The Role of the Holy Spirit | 45 |
| 7. Spiritual Growth and Maturity | 53 |
| 8. Community in Christ | 65 |

| | |
|---|---|
| 9. Mission and Purpose | 73 |
| 10. Complete in Christ | 81 |
| Conclusion | 89 |
| Appendices | 91 |

*To every woman, man, and young person
who will read this book.
My prayer is that you will not just
read words on a page,
but encounter the fullness of Christ
that changes everything.*

# Acknowledgements

This book has been many years in the making! I am grateful to God for His lovingkindness, tender mercies, and faithfulness, which have brought me to the place where I am today. He has inscribed the truth about my completeness in Him on my heart and I am forever grateful.

I acknowledge the love and patience of my mother, who has never ceased praying for me and supporting me in adverse times.

The practical journey to completeness often involves people, too many to mention by name. However, I am grateful for every spiritual mentor, pastor, and teacher whose voices helped shape my understanding of my identity in Christ. Your impact is woven into the fabric of this message.

With deep gratitude, I appreciate the Kingdom Love International Network (KLINE) and Unique Women family. Thank you for believing in the vision, for walking in love, and for growing together in truth. You are proof that God's grace builds a people for His glory.

This book would not be a reality today without my publisher, Pastor Tokunbo Emmanuel. Thank you for your guidance, expertise, and excellence, which shine through all the pages of this book.

To my dear husband, life partner, and covering, thank you for your patience, prayers, and unwavering support through the years of ministry and growth. You have been a true reflection of Christ's love to me.

To my children and family, thank you for allowing me space to follow God's call and for encouraging me with your words, prayers, and sacrifices.

## Author's Preface

In a world that constantly demands more from us – more achievement, more perfection, more validation – it is a deep comfort and truth to know that we are already complete in Christ. That is the heartbeat of this book.

*We Are Complete in Him* is not just the study of a single verse; it is an invitation to rediscover the power and peace of Colossians 2:10: *"And you are complete in Him, who is the head of all principality and power."* Over the years, this foundational truth has been liberating and transformative for me. It has helped me understand deeply that my identity, sufficiency, and calling are rooted in Christ alone.

As a woman, wife, mother, mentor, minister, and visionary leader, I have wrestled with seasons of emptiness, inadequacy, and self-doubt. But through the Word and the gentle guidance of the Holy Spirit, I encountered the liberating truth that everything I need

- identity, purpose, strength, love, healing, peace, and joy - is already mine in Christ Jesus.

This book is a call to rest in the finished work of Christ and to live from the place of divine sufficiency. Whether you're battling insecurity, shame, rejection, confusion, or weariness, I pray these pages will remind you that in Him, you lack nothing.

It is my prayer that by the time you finish this book, you will not only have understood the doctrine of spiritual completeness, but you will also be ready to live it out. This truth will permeate your faith, relationships, ministry, and mission. You will stand taller, love deeper, serve stronger, and walk freer... because you are complete in Him.

**Lydia Shola Olorunniwo**
*Founder, Kingdom Love International Network (KLINE)*

# Foreword

In an attempt to explain the dynamics of walking with God, theologians and teachers of biblical doctrine have used different words to encapsulate spiritual realities. When, through the confession of our faith in the sacrifice of Christ on the cross, the weight and burden of sin are rolled away, we understand that *we are saved*. From this point onward, the Father sees us through the eyes of Christ and declares that *we are justified*. Having now been saved by grace, we are taught to live our lives set apart for God and be in a place to say *we are sanctified*. Ultimately, we hope to one day confess that in Him *we are glorified*.

These teachings come in various shades and sizes. However, if the revelation of our completeness in Christ is not received as a cornerstone of faith, a subtle sense of needing to strive for His acceptance can sneak into the Christian walk. Such striving is often in the flesh and neglects the depth of God's love.

If God loved us whilst we were yet sinners, would the intensity of His love reduce now that He calls us His children? Maybe we need to come to Him as children, lay aside all striving, and confess the simple, yet profound truth that *we are complete in Him* – a completeness that grasps, by faith, that we are *already* saved, justified, sanctified, and glorified in Christ without to need to *earn* more of His love through our works.

This book will help us to do just that. It is not a theoretical treatise. Rather, it is the fruit of decades of yearning, learning, and submission to the inward working of the Holy Spirit. It fully unpacks the focal scripture, Colossians 2:10, and invites readers to experience the level of transformation that the author herself has known to be true in her life.

Our paths in life may be different, but our confession of faith should be the same: *We are complete in Christ!* May the Lord open our eyes to appreciate the treasures of wisdom that this book contains.

**Tokunbo Emmanuel**
*CEO, Sophos Books Ltd.*

# INTRODUCTION

Each chapter of *We Are Complete in Him* is crafted with a specific goal in mind: to draw you deeper into the richness of Christ and equip you to walk confidently in your identity. These goals include:

1. **Understanding Spiritual Completeness.** You will gain a solid grasp of what it means to be spiritually complete in Christ. Colossians 2:10 is not an abstract idea. It's a spiritual reality that shapes how we live. Paul echoes this in *Ephesians 1:3*, reminding us that we have already been blessed with every spiritual blessing in heavenly places. Likewise, *Philippians 4:19* reassures us that our every need is met in His glorious riches.

2. **Deepening Your Relationship with Christ.** This book will encourage you to move beyond religion into intimate communion

with Jesus, the One who completes us. Like branches connected to the vine (*John 15:5*), we draw life and strength from Him. As Paul declared in *Philippians 3:8-9*, knowing Christ is more valuable than anything else.

3. **Overcoming Feelings of Inadequacy.** Many believers live under the weight of "not enough." But in Christ, we lack nothing. Through the Word, you will learn to silence the voice of inadequacy and trust in God's sufficiency. *2 Corinthians 12:9* reminds us that His strength is perfected in our weakness. *Psalm 23:1* assures us that with the Lord as our Shepherd, we shall not want.

4. **Living a Transformed Life.** To be complete in Him is not just a doctrinal fact; it's a call to transformation. You will discover how this truth shapes your thinking, your habits, your relationships. *Romans 12:2* urges us not to conform but to be transformed, and *Galatians 2:20* points to a life wholly surrendered to Christ.

5. **Strengthening Faith Amid Challenges.**

Life's trials often tempt us to question our sufficiency, but even in hardship, we are complete in Him. This book will offer you strength and perspective for the storms of life. *James 1:2-4* encourages us to embrace trials with joy, knowing they produce spiritual maturity. And *Hebrews 12:2* directs our gaze to Jesus, the author and finisher of our faith.

6. **Encouraging Spiritual Growth and Maturity.** Completeness in Christ is not a destination; it is a journey of growing into the fullness we already possess. We'll explore how to mature in grace, walk in knowledge, and live out our calling. *Ephesians 4:13* calls us to grow into the stature of Christ, while *2 Peter 3:18* invites us to increase in grace and understanding.

7. **Embracing Unity in the Body of Christ.** Our completeness is a corporate reality. The Church, the Body of Christ, thrives when each part recognises its place and purpose. You will be stirred to love, serve, and build others up, contributing to the health of the whole. *1 Corinthians 12:12-13* and *Ephesians 4:16* anchor this call to unity.

8. **Equipping for Mission and Service.** As we grasp our identity in Christ, we are propelled into purpose. You will be encouraged to serve others with boldness and joy, sharing the message of wholeness in Christ to a broken world. *Matthew 28:19–20* commissions us, and *1 Peter 4:10* reminds us that every believer is gifted for impact.

# Setting the Stage

Long before social feeds and sound-bite sermons, a letter travelled from a Roman prison to a small, rather forgettable town called Colossae. Penned by Paul around A.D. 60-62, this epistle carried a blazing conviction: Christ is enough - entirely, exhaustively, eternally enough.

### 1. A Scroll from a Cell

Paul writes as a chained ambassador, yet his words roam free. Though he had never set foot in Colossae, his heart is pastorally invested in this young congregation. False teachers were peddling a spiritual "upgrade"-package, which included Judaism's rituals, Greek philosophy, early Gnostic whispers. Paul answers with a thunderclap: *"In Him dwells all the fullness of Deity... and you are complete in Him"* (Col 2:9-10).

## 2. A City Past Its Prime

Colossae, once a bustling node on the trade route, had faded beneath the shadows of flashier neighbours Laodicea and Hierapolis. Culturally, it was a collage of pagan temples, synagogues, and mystery cults. Into this swirl, a fledgling house-church tried to find its footing. Their greatest threat wasn't persecution; it was but confusion, the temptation to splice Christ with a bit of everything else.

## 3. Four Pulses of the Letter

- **The Supremacy of Christ** – Paul paints Christ as pre-eminent Creator and cosmic Head (1:15-20).

- **Fullness in Christ** – All the Godhead in bodily form, all believers complete in Him (2:9-10).

- **Warning Lights** – Hollow philosophies, rule-keeping, self-denial that masquerades as holiness (2:8,16-23).

- **Transformed Living** – New hearts, new habits, new household ethics (3:1-17).

## 4. Zooming In on Colossians 2:8-10

First, Paul flashes a red light: **"Don't be kidnapped by empty theory."** Then he raises the banner: **Christ contains all the fullness of God.** Finally, he delivers the triumphal shout: **"And you have been brought to that fullness!"** No additives, no spiritual growth hormones required.

## 5. Why This Verse Still Sparks Today

- **Modern Heresies, Ancient Remedy** – Legalism, relativism, syncretism: same old lies with shinier packaging. Col 2:10 undercuts them all.

- **Identity Detox** – In an age that measures worth by likes, titles, and trophies, this verse declares our value sealed in Christ.

- **Security for the Soul** – Completeness isn't a merit badge earned; it's a birthright received. That certainty breeds peace in turbulent times.

- **Everyday Outworking** – Completeness is

not complacency. It fuels growth, generosity, and resilient joy.

## 6. Living the Text

- **Personal Devotion** – Prayer, Scripture, worship become the daily reminder: *I lack nothing in Him.*

- **Community Synergy** – A church that knows its completeness stops competing and starts completing one another.

- **Missional Overflow** – We evangelise, not to fix our deficits, but to share our surplus—inviting a fractured world into wholeness.

To grasp the **context** of Colossians 2:10 is to feel the weight of Paul's chain rattle across centuries, reminding us:

*Christ plus nothing equals everything.* As you turn the pages ahead, let this ancient proclamation seep into modern veins, steadying your heart against counterfeit cures and propelling you to live boldly from the fullness already yours – *complete in Him.*

# 1

## UNDERSTANDING COMPLETENESS

### BIBLICAL AND THEOLOGICAL FOUNDATIONS

Before we explore how to live out our spiritual fullness, we must first understand what "completeness" means, biblically and theologically. This chapter lays that foundation, showing how the concept stretches across Scripture and finds its fulfilment in Christ.

## Completeness in the Old Testament: The Shalom of God

In the Hebrew Scriptures, completeness is wrapped in the word *shalom,* a word far richer than "peace." It conveys wholeness, wellness, nothing missing, nothing broken. When Isaiah declares, *"You keep him in perfect peace whose mind is stayed on You"* (Isaiah 26:3), he is speaking of a mind anchored in God's wholeness. Similarly, David's bold statement in Psalm 23:1, *"The*

*Lord is my shepherd; I shall not want,"* echoes the same truth: in God's care, we lack nothing. Completeness was always God's intention for His people.

## New Testament Fulfilment: Fullness in Christ

The New Testament unveils this Old Testament shadow in the person of Jesus. The Greek word *plērōma*, meaning "fullness," appears prominently in Colossians 2:9-10: *"In Christ all the fullness of the Deity lives in bodily form, and in Him you have been brought to fullness."* Jesus isn't just a messenger, He is the message, the fulfilment of every divine promise. As He says in Matthew 5:17, *"I have not come to abolish [the Law or the Prophets], but to fulfil them."*

## Union with Christ: Position and Privilege

Theologically, this completeness is rooted in our union with Christ. When we are "in Him," we share in His life, His righteousness, His inheritance. Paul puts it plainly in Galatians 2:20: *"It is no longer I who live, but Christ lives in me."* Through this union, we are declared righteous, not because of our merit but because of Christ's sacrifice. *"In Him we become the righteousness of God"* (2 Corinthians 5:21).

## The Sufficiency of Christ

Christ's sufficiency means that He is not just the starting point of our spiritual journey, He is the entire path. John writes, *"From His fullness we have all received, grace upon grace"* (John 1:16). Ephesians 1:3 echoes the abundance: *"He has blessed us with every spiritual blessing in the heavenly realms."* Nothing is withheld. Nothing is lacking.

## Sanctification: A Process of Becoming

Our completeness in Christ is both a finished work and a continuing process. Positionally, we are complete at salvation. Practically, we are being transformed day by day. As Paul writes in Philippians 1:6, *"He who began a good work in you will bring it to completion."* This journey of maturing in faith is what Paul describes in Colossians 1:28, presenting every believer "mature in Christ."

## Living from Identity, Not for It

Grasping our completeness reshapes how we view ourselves. No longer defined by performance or pain, our identity is rooted in Christ. *"We are His workmanship,"* says Ephesians 2:10, God's masterpiece, designed with purpose. And because there is no condemnation for those in Christ (Romans 8:1), we are free to live without fear or shame.

## Empowered for Abundance

Completeness empowers. We are equipped for good works (2 Timothy 3:17), called to live the abundant life Christ promised (John 10:10). Peace, joy, purpose, these are not reserved for the spiritually elite. They are the inheritance of every believer.

## Barriers to Understanding Completeness

Culture often clouds our view. Messages of self-sufficiency and perfectionism pull us away from dependence on Christ. Jeremiah 17:5 warns against trusting in human strength. Jesus, instead, offers rest to the weary (Matthew 11:28–30). We must also guard against legalism - rituals that replace relationship –

as well as false teachings that distort Christ's finished work (Colossians 2:16–17; 1 John 4:1).

Completeness in Christ is not just a theological idea; it's the truth we stand on, live from, and grow into.

## The Fullness of Christ: Attributes That Make Us Whole

If we are complete in Him, we must ask: who is He? What is it about Christ that makes Him the source of our fullness? In this chapter, we explore His divine attributes, each one a fountain of spiritual completeness.

### Christ's Deity

Paul's words in Colossians 2:9 are uncompromising: *"In Him all the fullness of Deity dwells in bodily form."* Jesus is not a reflection of God—He is God. John 1 makes this explicit: *"The Word was God... and the Word became flesh."* Our completeness rests not in a teacher or prophet, but in the God-Man.

### His Power and Authority

Christ's omnipotence ensures there is no need He cannot meet. *"All authority in heaven and on earth has been given to Me,"* He declares (Matthew 28:18). Hebrews 1:3 affirms that He upholds all things by the power of His word. That's the kind of power that holds us together.

## His Infinite Knowledge

We are not hidden from Him. Christ's omniscience means He knows us intimately—our fears, our flaws, our frame. He sees what we cannot and guides us with perfect wisdom (John 16:30; Psalm 139:1-4).

## His Ever-Present Help

Christ is not distant. His omnipresence means He is with us always (Matthew 28:20). Wherever we go, His hand leads, His presence comforts (Psalm 139:7-10).

## His Unchanging Nature

In a world where everything shifts, Christ is constant. *"Jesus Christ is the same yesterday, today, and forever"* (Hebrews 13:8). This immutability gives us a sure foundation because His promises never expire.

## His Perfect Holiness

Christ is holy, pure, unstained. He calls us to share in that holiness—not by striving, but by yielding. *"Be holy, for I am holy"* (1 Peter 1:15-16). His holiness both convicts and empowers.

## His Boundless Love

Love is not just what Christ does; it's who He is. *"While we were still sinners, Christ died for us"* (Romans 5:8). This love fills every void and empowers us to love in return (Ephesians 3:18-19).

## His Overflowing Grace

Grace is the fragrance of Christ's fullness. It meets us in weakness, sustains us in trials, and trains us in godliness (2 Corinthians 12:9; Titus 2:11-12). We are saved by grace and we live by grace.

## His Eternal Truth

Christ is not one truth among many. He is *the* Truth (John 14:6). His truth sets us free (John 8:32) and anchors us in a world of shifting narratives.

## His Infinite Wisdom

In Christ are hidden all treasures of wisdom and knowledge (Colossians 2:3). His counsel never fails, His timing never errs, His insight never misses. We can trust His leadership in every season (James 1:5).

Knowing these attributes draws us into deeper worship and stronger trust. Far from just being theological descriptions, they are the pillars of our spiritual completeness.

## Human vs. Spiritual Completeness: A Revealing Comparison

The world offers a definition of completeness that sounds appealing—but it's hollow. In contrast, Scripture offers a deeper, richer, more lasting completeness found only in Christ.

## The Illusion of Self-Sufficiency

The culture champions independence: "Be enough. Do enough. Need no one." But this illusion often leads to isolation, pressure, and pride. Stories of self-made success can inspire, but they rarely satisfy. Jeremiah

17:5 issues a sobering reminder: *"Cursed is the one who trusts in man."*

## The Chase of Material Success

We are told completeness lies in possessions, promotions, or prestige. But these fade. The "American Dream" is a treadmill, not a destination. Many find that the more they gain, the more they feel something's still missing.

## The Pursuit of Personal Fulfilment

Happiness, romance, self-actualisation, and other phenomena are the new idols of modern completeness. While these can be gifts, they are poor gods. Circumstantial fulfilment is fragile. The soul needs something eternal.

## The Biblical Vision of Completeness

In contrast, spiritual completeness is rooted in **union with Christ**. He is the vine; we are the branches (John 15:4). He gives us not only identity, but security, peace, and purpose. Fulfilment is no longer based on what we achieve, but on what we've received. As Paul says, *"I *have learned to be content... I can do all things through Him"* (Philippians 4:11-13).

## What's Permanent, What's Not

Human completeness is temporary, subject to economic downturns, relational breakdowns, and physical decline. But spiritual completeness is unshakable. Christ is our rock. Our identity in Him does not shift with seasons.

## Living Differently, Thinking Eternally

Embracing spiritual completeness leads to transformed living. We shift from striving to resting. We serve others not from lack but from overflow. We reevaluate priorities, seek eternal values, and ground our worth not in applause but in adoption.

When we contrast human and spiritual completeness, we are confronted with a choice: pursue fleeting satisfaction, or embrace eternal wholeness. The world offers fragments; Christ offers fullness.

# 2

# THE DEITY OF CHRIST

To understand what it means to be complete in Christ, we must first understand who Christ is. At the heart of our spiritual fullness lies a foundational truth: Jesus Christ is fully God. His divine nature, supreme authority, and eternal roles as Creator and Redeemer are not mere theological statements—they are the very reasons we lack nothing in Him.

## Christ the Head: Supreme Over All

When Paul writes in Colossians 2:10, *"He is the head over every power and authority,"* he's making a bold declaration about Christ's supremacy. Christ isn't simply one voice among many; He stands above all rulers, systems, and forces. His authority is absolute.

For the believer, this brings deep assurance. No opposition, whether demonic or human, can undo the authority of Christ. Ephesians 1:22–23 echoes this truth: *"God placed all things under His feet and appointed Him to be head over everything for the church... the fullness of Him who fills everything in every way."*

When we recognise Christ's supreme headship, our response must be one of humble **submission** and **confidence**. We align our lives with His lordship, not as a burden, but as a safeguard. When Christ is at the centre, everything else finds its proper place.

## The Fullness of Deity in Human Form

Colossians 2:9 takes us deeper: *"For in Him all the fullness of Deity dwells in bodily form."* This single verse is a theological wellspring. Jesus is not just a representative of God; He is God. Fully divine, fully human, He embodies the fullness of the Godhead in a form we can know, follow, and love.

This truth affirms the triune nature of God. Jesus is not less than the Father or separate from the Spirit. He is co-equal, co-eternal, and co-existent within the Trinity. As John 1 declares, *"In the beginning was the Word... and the Word became flesh and dwelt among us."*

And here's the implication for us: *if Christ is fully God, then He is fully sufficient.* There is no spiritual need we can have that falls outside the scope of His power or grace. In Him, we have access to the entire reservoir of divine wisdom, strength, and blessing. We do not need to look elsewhere for completion. Christ is our Source.

## Creator and Redeemer: Anchors of Our Identity

To be complete in Christ is to be deeply connected to His two foundational roles: Creator and Redeemer.

As Creator, He is the origin and sustainer of all things. Paul writes in Colossians 1:16–17, *"All things were created by Him and for Him... in Him all things hold together."* This means your existence is not accidental. You were made by Christ, for Christ, and your meaning is tied to His mission. Knowing this reshapes how we see our worth and purpose.

As Redeemer, Christ rescues and restores. His deity makes His sacrifice infinitely effective, only God could bear the full weight of sin and rise victorious. *"In Him we have redemption through His blood,"* Paul writes in Ephesians 1:7. Through His death and resurrection, we are forgiven and made whole. Our past is covered, our present is empowered, and our eternity is secured.

Redemption restores relationship. The barrier of sin is broken, and fellowship with God is fully restored. More than that, the indwelling presence of Christ transforms us from the inside out, leading us on the journey of sanctification, growing more into His likeness each day.

## Living in the Reality of His Deity

Understanding the deity of Christ will elevate our theology and revolutionise our daily lives.

When we truly grasp that Christ is fully God, our hearts respond with **worship and reverence**. Philippians 2 reminds us that at His name, every knee will bow and every tongue confess His lordship. We don't just admire Jesus; we adore Him, honour Him, and submit our lives to Him.

This revelation also stirs **trust**. If Christ is God, then He is able, and willing, to meet every need. *"His divine power has given us everything we need for life and godliness,"* says 2 Peter 1:3. We don't live in fear or scarcity. We walk in faith, resting in His sufficiency.

And finally, His deity compels us to proclaim His name. The Great Commission flows from Christ's authority: *"All authority in heaven and on earth has been given to Me. Go, therefore…"* (Matthew 28:18–20). We share the gospel not as a suggestion, but as a response to divine command, telling the world that the fullness they seek is found in Christ alone.

To know that Christ is God is to know that we are complete in Him. His authority secures us, His fullness sustains us, His roles define us, and His presence transforms us. This is the foundation of our identity, and the reason we can live with bold assurance: we are complete, because He is.

# 3

# OUR IDENTITY IN CHRIST

LIVING FROM WHOLENESS, NOT FOR IT

One of the greatest revelations in the life of a believer is this: *we do not earn or create our identity, we receive our identity through faith.* In Christ, we are not trying to become someone; we are discovering who we already are. Our spiritual completeness is deeply rooted in this identity. When we understand who we are in Him, we begin to live not from deficit, but from abundance.

## Born Again, Made New

Scripture is unequivocal: *"If anyone is in Christ, he is a new creation. The old has passed away; behold, the new has come"* (2 Corinthians 5:17). This is a powerful spiritual reality. To be in Christ is to be fundamentally changed. We are not simply improved or upgraded; we are reborn.

This newness springs from a divine work. It begins with *regeneration* the moment the Holy Spirit breathes new life into our spirit (John 3:3–7). It is affirmed by *justification*, where God declares us righteous, not because of our works but because of Christ's righteousness (Romans 5:1). And it continues through *sanctification,* the ongoing, Spirit-empowered process of being conformed to Christ's image (1 Thessalonians 4:3–4).

The implications are staggering. As new creations, we are no longer defined by sin, shame, or striving. We are set free from the power of sin (Romans 6:6–7), and our hearts are rewired with new desires, bearing the fruit of the Spirit, which is love, joy, peace, and more (Galatians 5:22–23).

## One with Christ: The Mystery of Union

At the centre of our new identity lies the mystery of **union with Christ**. This isn't just metaphorical; it is a living, spiritual connection. Paul's letter to the Ephesians overflows with this truth: we are adopted, redeemed, sealed, and given an eternal inheritance because we are "in Christ" (Ephesians 1:3–14).

This union is both mystical and practical. Spiritually, it means that we are joined to Jesus in a way that transcends understanding. As He said in John 15, we are branches connected to the Vine, dependent on Him for life, growth, and fruitfulness. *"Apart from Me,"* He says, *"you can do nothing."*

Practically, it means we abide in Him daily, drawing strength, guidance, and identity from His presence. Our union bears fruit in every area of life (John 15:8), and leads us into deeper intimacy with Him. As Paul longed in Philippians 3:10, we come to know Christ personally.

This union also redefines our story. In Christ's death, our old self was buried. In His resurrection, we rose to new life (Romans 6:3–4). Baptism proclaims this truth outwardly, but inwardly, it marks the beginning of a brand-new identity.

## Living From Who We Are

Knowing who we are in Christ is one thing. Living from that identity is another. This is where transformation takes root, going beyond head knowledge and becoming a daily application of truth.

The first battleground is the **mind**. *"Do not be conformed to this world,"* Paul writes, *"but be transformed by the renewing of your mind"* (Romans 12:2). This renewal happens as we immerse ourselves in Scripture, letting God's Word reshape our thoughts and beliefs (Colossians 3:16). It's not a one-time switch; it's a daily discipline, a reprogramming of the soul.

From a renewed mind comes a Spirit-led walk. Paul instructs us to *"walk by the Spirit,"* which means living in daily surrender to the Holy Spirit's leading (Galatians 5:16). This walk results in the transformation of our character, bearing the fruit of compassion, humility, patience, and love, qualities that don't come naturally, but grow in us as we remain in Christ (Colossians 3:12–14; 2 Peter 1:5–7).

Living from our identity also means embracing our divine calling. Ephesians 2:10 reminds us that we are *"God's workmanship, created in Christ Jesus for good works."* Our completeness in Christ is not passive; it is purposeful. God has uniquely gifted us to serve others, and as we do, we reflect His fullness to the world (1 Peter 4:10).

## Walking in Community and Mission

Identity in Christ is not only personal, it is also communal. We are not lone branches; we are part of a body. Scripture calls us to meet, encourage, challenge, and support one another (Hebrews 10:24–25; Acts 2:42).

In community, our identity is strengthened. In fellowship, our completeness is expressed.

And because we are secure in who we are, we can now live **missionally**. We are not begging the world for validation; we are offering it the love of God. Jesus sends us into the world to make disciples (Matthew 28:19–20), and Paul calls us ambassadors of reconciliation (2 Corinthians 5:20). Sharing the gospel is a natural overflow of knowing we've been made whole.

When we truly embrace our identity in Christ, we no longer live from fear or striving. We walk confidently, knowing who we are and whose we are. We are not defined by our past or our performance. We are defined by grace, secured by love, and empowered by truth.

We are complete in Him, and this changes everything.

# 4

# WHEN STRENGTH FAILS, GRACE PREVAILS

There's something humbling about confronting our own limitations. The ache of failure, the sting of sin, the slow, silent wrestle with doubts we dare not speak aloud; all these whisper the same haunting refrain: *You are not enough*. And in truth, we aren't.

Scripture does not flatter us in this regard. "For He knows our frame; He remembers that we are dust" (Psalm 103:14). We are frail, only held together by grace. The body tires. The mind frays. The spirit stumbles. From the sudden grip of illness to the silent fog of depression, from gnawing anxiety to lurking temptation, our frailty shows up in countless forms.

Yet frailty alone is not our only problem. Beneath it lies a deeper fracture – *sin*. "For all have sinned and fall short of the glory of God" (Romans 3:23). Sin is more than failure; it is rebellion, a turning away from our Creator's design. It separates us from God, births shame, ruptures relationships, and eventually leads to spiritual death (Romans 6:23). It is the root of our incompleteness, and no amount of self-help can close the chasm it creates.

Like Paul, we cry out: *"Wretched man that I am! Who will deliver me from this body of death?"* (Romans 7:24). But thanks be to God! The answer is not found in trying harder, but in trusting deeper. "Thanks be to God through Jesus Christ our Lord!"

## Christ, Our Enough

Into the void of our not-enoughness steps the All-Sufficient One. Christ is not merely an addition to our lives; He is our life (Colossians 3:4). Where we are weak, He is strong. Where we fall short, He fills the gap.

He lived the life we could not live, sinless, yet sympathetic. "We do not have a high priest who is unable to sympathise with our weaknesses," the writer of Hebrews reminds us, "but one who in every respect has been tempted as we are, yet without sin" (Hebrews 4:15). Christ knows the weight of temptation, but unlike us, He bore it without ever yielding.

He died the death we deserved. "For our sake, He made Him to be sin who knew no sin, so that in Him we might become the righteousness of God" (2

Corinthians 5:21). On the cross, Jesus took our shame and gave us His righteousness. Through His sacrifice, we are not merely patched up, we are made new.

And He rose again triumphantly, victorious over the grave. The same power that raised Christ now works in us (Philippians 3:10). His indwelling presence, "Christ in you, the hope of glory" (Colossians 1:27), is not symbolic, it is real. He strengthens. He leads. He remains.

We are never alone in our weakness because the fullness of Christ lives within us..

## Walking in Completeness

But how do we live this out? How do we take this divine truth and turn it into daily rhythm?

### 1. Living by Faith

Faith is not wishful thinking; it is a settled confidence in Christ's sufficiency. Paul put it this way: *"I have been crucified with Christ... and the life I now live in the flesh I live by faith in the Son of God"* (Galatians 2:20). Each day, we wake up not in our own strength, but in His. Even when we feel weak, His grace is sufficient; His power is made perfect in our imperfection (2 Corinthians 12:9).

## 2. Leaning into Prayer

Prayer is not a ritual; it is relationship. It is where our weakness meets His strength. "Do not be anxious about anything," Paul writes, "but in everything... let your requests be made known to God" (Philippians 4:6–7). In prayer, we pour out our weariness and receive His peace. And when we don't know what to pray, the Spirit intercedes with groanings too deep for words (Romans 8:26–27).

## 3. Committing to Discipleship

To grow in Christlikeness is not a solo endeavour. Jesus commands us to make disciples, but we must also be discipled. Through teaching, correction, encouragement, and example, we grow. And we help others grow (2 Timothy 2:2). It's how the body is built, one life sharpening another.

## 4. Embracing Community

No one becomes complete in Christ alone. The Christian journey was never meant to be walked in isolation. "Let us not give up meeting together," Hebrews urges, "but encourage one another, and all the more as you see the Day approaching" (Hebrews 10:24–25). In the fellowship of believers, we find strength, accountability, and love that lifts us when we fall.

**5. Cultivating Spiritual Disciplines**
Finally, growth requires training. "Train yourself for godliness," Paul tells Timothy, "for while bodily training is of some value, godliness is of value in every way" (1 Timothy 4:7–8). Through disciplines like Scripture meditation, fasting, worship, and silence, we make space for grace to work deeply in us. These are not burdens; they are blessings. They don't earn us completeness; they help us embrace it.

## In Him, We Are Made Whole

Human frailty and sin may shout of our insufficiency, but they are not the final word. Christ is. His voice cuts through the noise of shame and declares us whole. Not by our strength, but by His sacrifice. Not by our perfection, but by His grace.

This chapter is not merely an invitation to acknowledge your weakness, it is a summons to embrace Christ's strength. To step out of striving and into abiding. To trade your brokenness for His beauty. And to walk, step by step, in the completeness that is already yours... in Him.

## 5

## THE POWER OF THE CROSS

There is no Christian completeness without the cross of Jesus. The cross stands at the centre of our faith. It is not as a mere symbol of suffering, but the place where justice met mercy, and sinners are made saints. It is where heaven's love paid the full price for earth's rebellion. Through the cross, we were redeemed, restored, and raised into a new identity. And through the cross, we are empowered to walk in daily victory.

This chapter unveils how the cross secures our completeness and shows us how to live in its power every single day.

# The Cross That Bought Our Freedom

*"In Him we have redemption through His blood, the forgiveness of our trespasses, according to the riches of His grace."*
**(Ephesians 1:7)**

To redeem is to buy back; to set free at a cost. In biblical terms, humanity was not merely misguided; we were enslaved to sin. And the price of freedom was blood. Not silver or gold. Not effort or penance. But the precious blood of Christ, poured out on the cross for us (Mark 10:45).

Redemption was not a divine afterthought. It was always the plan. From the first Passover lamb whose blood shielded God's people from judgment (Exodus 12), to the kinsman-redeemer Boaz who bought Ruth's future and gave her a name, the Old Testament pointed forward to the One who would redeem us from spiritual ruin. Jesus, the true Lamb of God (John 1:29), fulfilled it all.

## Atoned by Love

> *"He entered once for all into the holy places... by means of His own blood, thus securing an eternal redemption."*
> **(Hebrews 9:12)**

Atonement speaks of restoration, a broken relationship made whole. Through His death, Jesus took our sin upon Himself and made peace between us and God.

This was divine substitution. He bore our punishment (Isaiah 53:5). He satisfied the justice of God (1 John 2:2). He reconciled us back into divine fellowship (Colossians 1:20).

Because of the cross:

- We are *forgiven:* the guilt of sin is gone (Romans 8:1).

- We are *freed:* sin no longer rules over us (Romans 6:6).

- We are *family:* adopted as sons and daughters (Galatians 4:4–7).

# Victory Over Sin and Death: The Cross That Changed Everything

> *"For sin will have no dominion over you, since you are not under law but under grace."*
> **(Romans 6:14)**

The cross does more than pardon us from sin; it empowers us to overcome sin and live a new life – Christ's life.

Jesus didn't just die *for* us; He lives *in* us. And His victory becomes ours. By His wounds we are healed and strengthened to stand. Sin may knock, but it no longer owns the key. When temptation comes, we resist not in our strength, but in His (James 4:7).

In Christ, we are no longer defined by our past, our habits, or our shame. We are new creations, with new appetites, new strength, and a new name (2 Corinthians 5:17).

## Death Has Lost Its Sting

> *"O death, where is your victory? O death, where is your sting?... Thanks be to God, who gives us the victory through our Lord Jesus Christ."*
> **(1 Corinthians 15:55–57)**

The cross not only defeats sin; it conquers death.

At Calvary, death was swallowed up in victory. Jesus rose, not just to prove a point, but to secure a promise: eternal life for all who believe (John 11:25–26). Death, once feared, is now a doorway, an entry into unbroken fellowship with God (Philippians 1:21).

One day, even our mortal bodies will become incorruptible, glorious, and eternal (1 Corinthians 15:42–44). The cross made that possible.

## Living in the Power of the Cross

> *"I have been crucified with Christ. It is no longer I who live, but Christ who lives in me..."*
> **(Galatians 2:20)**

Christ didn't die so we could live *almost* free. He died to birth a brand-new way of living. We die to the old and rise to the new. Our values shift and our habits change. Our day-to-day decisions bear eternal weight.

As Paul urged, we put to death what belongs to the earthly nature (Colossians 3:5), and we clothe ourselves in Christ (Colossians 3:10). Day by day, we grow into who we already are, complete in Him.

## Walking in Daily Victory

> *"In all these things we are more than conquerors through Him who loved us."*
> **(Romans 8:37)**

Victory is not reserved for special moments; it's meant for everyday life.

- *Faith over fear:* We reject worry, knowing we are covered (2 Timothy 1:7).

- *Scripture and prayer:* Our daily weapons against temptation (Ephesians 6:10–18).

- *Walking in the Spirit:* Choosing God's will over fleshly impulses (Galatians 5:16).

This is a call to pursue perfection, made possible by the cross.

## Sharing the Message of the Cross

The cross is too powerful to be kept secret .It's not just our foundation; it's our life message. We preach Christ crucified. We live as walking witnesses. Our lives reflect His love, our words echo His grace, and our presence points to His glory. Jesus commissioned us to "Go therefore and make disciples..." (Matthew 28:19–20).

We are not just recipients of the cross; we are *ambassadors* of its power (2 Corinthians 5:20).

## The Cross Is Our Completeness

The cross is not a one-time event. It is an ever-present reality.

It redeems us. It defeats sin and death. It empowers our every step.

The power of the cross is not limited to Sunday sermons or Easter celebrations. It is the bedrock of our identity, the fuel for our journey, and the assurance of our future. In the cross, we are forgiven and made whole.

So let us live not as people trying to earn completeness, but as those who already have it, because Christ was willing to bleed for it.

# 6

# THE ROLE OF THE HOLY SPIRIT

You cannot talk about completeness in Christ without talking about the Holy Spirit. He is not an accessory to the Christian life; He is the breath in our lungs, the whisper in our conscience, the fire in our bones. Jesus didn't merely save us and leave us; He sent the Spirit to dwell in us, lead us, transform us, and empower us for holy living. Without the Spirit, we are dry bones; with Him, we are fully alive.

In this chapter, we explore how the Holy Spirit completes the work of Christ in us and through us, making us vessels of divine life and fruit.

## God's Presence Within Us

*"I will ask the Father, and He will give you another Helper... even the Spirit of truth... He dwells with you and will be in you."*
**(John 14:16–17)**

When Jesus spoke these words, He was declaring the very heart of the new covenant. The Holy Spirit would not merely come upon people for a task. He would take up permanent residence within us.

At salvation, the Spirit becomes our seal (Ephesians 1:13–14), a down payment of our inheritance and the unmistakable sign that we belong to Christ. "Anyone who does not have the Spirit of Christ does not belong to Him" (Romans 8:9). His presence in us is essential.

## The Spirit: Source of Our Completeness

*"In Him you have been made complete..."*
**(Colossians 2:10)**

How does the Spirit complete us?
- *Regeneration:* He gives us new birth and a spiritual awakening (Titus 3:5).

- *Sanctification:* He steadily transforms us into Christ's image (2 Corinthians 3:18).

- *Empowerment:* He strengthens us to say "no" to sin and "yes" to righteousness (Romans 8:13).

- *Assurance:* He testifies within us that we are children of God (Romans 8:16).

The Spirit of Christ within changes our behaviour and rewrites our identity. We are no longer orphans or wanderers. We are sons and daughters, heirs of the Kingdom (Romans 8:15). And when we cry, "Abba, Father," it is the Spirit praying through us.

## A Spirit-Led Life

Jesus said, "When the Spirit of truth comes, He will guide you into all the truth..." (John 16:13). The world shouts a thousand confusing voices. But the Spirit speaks with clarity and conviction. He reveals the truth of Scripture, opening our eyes to what the natural mind cannot grasp (1 Corinthians 2:12–14). He leads us gently, even in life's crossroads, whispering, *"This is the way; walk in it"* (Isaiah 30:21).

He is also our divine conscience. He convicts us, not to shame, but to change. He exposes the lies we believe and redirects us to the light (John 16:8).

## Empowered for Holy Living

*"You will receive power when the Holy Spirit has come upon you..."*
**(Acts 1:8)**

The Christian life is impossible without the Spirit, and beautifully possible with Him.

- He gives us power to resist temptation (Galatians 5:16).

- He strengthens us through hardship, even when words fail (Romans 8:26).

- He equips us with gifts — wisdom, healing, discernment, prophecy — for building up the Body (1 Corinthians 12:4–11).

- He helps us pray when we don't know how (Romans 8:26–27).

The Spirit is not a passive presence. He is an active force — bold, loving, and wise.

## Keeping in Step with the Spirit

"If we live by the Spirit, let us also keep in step with the Spirit." (Galatians 5:25)

Walking with the Spirit is not about striving; it's about surrender.

- We **yield** our will each day to His.

- We **listen** for His voice, in the Word, in prayer, in stillness.

- We **trust** His strength over our own.

To keep in step is to dance to His rhythm, one obedient step at a time.

# The Fruit of the Spirit: Heaven's Evidence in Earthly Lives

*"But the fruit of the Spirit is love, joy, peace, patience, kindness..."*
**(Galatians 5:22–23)**

Fruit doesn't scream; it speaks. Quietly, steadily, it proves that something alive is growing within.

The **gifts** of the Spirit show what we do. The **fruit** of the Spirit shows who we are.

And each attribute of this fruit is a glimpse into Christlikeness:

- **Love**: The kind that lays down its life (John 13:34–35).

- **Joy**: That defies trials (Philippians 4:4).

- **Peace**: That stills the storm within (Philippians 4:7).

- **Patience**: That bears with others and endures delay (James 1:2–4).

- **Kindness**: That reflects God's mercy in action (Ephesians 4:32).

- **Goodness**: That walks with integrity (Titus 2:7–8).

- **Faithfulness**: That clings to God's promises (Hebrews 10:23).

- **Gentleness**: That chooses humility over harshness (Colossians 3:12).

- **Self-Control**: That governs the flesh with spiritual strength (2 Timothy 1:7).

This is what spiritual maturity looks like: fruit that lasts.

## Cultivating the Fruit

*"Abide in Me, and I in you... whoever abides in Me bears much fruit..."*
**(John 15:4–5)**

Fruit comes by abiding in Christ.
- We **remain** in Christ through prayer, worship,

and the Word.

- We **yield** to the Spirit instead of resisting Him.
- We **remove** the weights and sins that entangle us (Hebrews 12:1–2).

Growth is slow, but it is sure; and the world will taste and see that the Lord is good through our lives.

## The Spirit Makes Us Whole

The Holy Spirit is the very life of God within us. He indwells us, completes us, guides us, empowers us, and bears fruit through us. He whispers identity. He ignites passion. He moulds character. He is the breath of our completeness in Christ.

So let us not grieve Him, quench Him, or ignore Him. Let us **walk in step**, live in power, and bear His fruit, because where the Spirit of the Lord is, there is freedom... and fullness (2 Corinthians 3:17).

# 7

## SPIRITUAL GROWTH AND MATURITY

Salvation is the beginning of our journey in Christ, not its end. We are saved in a moment, but we are made mature over a lifetime. This process of spiritual growth is the beautiful, sometimes painful, transformation of becoming more like Jesus. It's not automatic, and it's never complete this side of eternity, but it is glorious. It requires our surrender, the Spirit's power, and a willingness to keep pressing on through every stage, season, and struggle.

This chapter explores the path from spiritual infancy to maturity, the tools that fuel our growth, and the challenges we overcome along the way.

# Stages of Spiritual Growth: From Milk to Maturity

Just as a child grows through stages of development, so does the believer. Scripture gives us images of spiritual infancy, adolescence, and adulthood to help us locate where we are, and what we need to grow into wholeness in Christ.

## 1. Spiritual Infancy: The New Believer

> *"Like newborn infants, long for the pure spiritual milk, that by it you may grow up into salvation."*
> **(1 Peter 2:2)**

New believers are full of wonder and zeal. They can also be vulnerable. They're learning to crawl in faith, discovering the basics of prayer, Scripture, and community. Yet like infants, they need nourishment, guidance, and protection.

**Common struggles** include confusion, emotional highs and lows, and temptation to return to old habits.

But growth comes through the Word (Matthew 4:4), through connection to mature believers (Hebrews 10:24–25), and through cultivating a daily rhythm of prayer (Colossians 4:2).

## 2. Spiritual Childhood: Learning and Growing

> *"For though by this time you ought to be teachers, you need someone to teach you again the basic principles..."*
> **(Hebrews 5:12)**

In this stage, believers are learning obedience and spiritual responsibility. They begin to grasp who they are in Christ and trust God in more areas of life. Yet there's still evidences of inconsistency, a tug-of-war between flesh and Spirit, knowledge and practice.

This is the time to dive deeper into Scripture (Joshua 1:8), apply faith in real-life trials (James 1:2–4), and begin actively serving God in small ways (James 1:22).

## 3. Spiritual Adolescence: Strength and Stretching

> *"I write to you, young men, because you are strong, and the word of God abides in you..."*
> **(1 John 2:14)**

Now the believer is stronger in the Word, sharper in discernment, and more aware of spiritual warfare. There's a sense of calling and conviction, together with a new intensity of testing.

This season requires deeper spiritual practices: fasting, worship, and perseverance through pain (Romans 5:3–5). It's also a time to both *receive mentorship* and *begin mentoring others* (2 Timothy 2:2). The adolescent in faith begins to fight not only for their own growth, but for the growth of others.

## 4. Spiritual Maturity: Christlikeness as the Goal

*"...to mature manhood, to the measure of the stature of the fullness of Christ."*
**(Ephesians 4:13)**

The spiritually mature believer walks with wisdom and grace. They're not easily shaken. They bear fruit consistently. They disciple others, serve with humility, and live with eternity in view.

Yet even at this stage, maturity is not static. The temptation now is complacency. But true maturity keeps pressing forward (Philippians 3:12–14), staying hungry for truth, and rooted in humility.

## Tools for Growth: Nourishment for the Soul

Spiritual maturity doesn't happen by chance. Like a strong tree, it must be watered, pruned, and fed. These four tools are the essential rhythms of growth:

## 1. Scripture: Our Daily Bread

*"All Scripture is breathed out by God... for training in righteousness."*
**(2 Timothy 3:16–17)**

The Word is the believer's lifeline, functioning like a mirror, a lamp, a sword, and a seed. It teaches, corrects, guides, and transforms. It renews our minds and anchors our hearts in truth (Psalm 119:11, James 1:22).

The following practical habits are essential for growth in God's Word:

- Follow a daily Bible reading plan.

- Study in-depth with commentaries and tools.

- Meditate and pray through Scripture for heart-level change.

## 2. Prayer: Staying in Constant Communion

*"In everything by prayer and supplication... let your requests be made known to God."*
**(Philippians 4:6–7)**

Prayer is not a religious ritual; it is the heart of our relationship with the living God. Through prayer, we draw close to the Father, gain peace, receive wisdom, and build intimacy with God.

Practical habits that will enrich your prayer life include the following:

- Set aside quiet time daily.

- Keep a prayer journal to track growth and answered prayers.

- Pray with others regularly for encouragement and agreement.

## 3. Community: Growing Together

*"Let us consider how to stir up one another to love and good works..."*
**(Hebrews 10:24–25)**

Growth happens best in the garden of godly relationships. We were never meant to grow alone. The church is where we learn, serve, are corrected, and are built up in love.

Embrace these Practical habits:
- Join a Bible study or small group.

- Develop relationships with mentors and spiritual friends.

- Be both a disciple and a discipler.

## 4. Service: Strengthening by Giving

> *"For even the Son of Man came not to be served, but to serve..."*
> **(Mark 10:45)**

Nothing stretches and strengthens our faith like service. As we pour out, God pours in. Ministry builds both spiritual and emotional muscle.

Practical habits for maximising the benefits of community include:
- Serve in your local church or community.

- Discover and use your spiritual gifts.

- Let every act of kindness be a gospel seed.

## Challenges and Triumphs: Growing Through Struggle

Some of the common challenges that believers encounter in their walk with God include the following:

- *Spiritual dryness:* when God feels distant.

- *Doubt and discouragement:* when our faith feels fragile.

- *Temptation:* the flesh battles the Spirit.

- *Spiritual warfare:* the enemy resists our growth.

Even these are part of the process. Growth is hardly ever a straight line; rather it's a winding road of valleys and peaks.

## Overcoming Obstacles

> *"Count it all joy... when you meet trials... for you know that the testing of your faith produces steadfastness."*
> **(James 1:2–4)**

Keep pressing in:
- Anchor yourself in the Word and prayer.
- Stay connected to spiritual community.
- Recall God's past faithfulness as fuel for present perseverance.

## The Fruit of Maturity

- A deeper walk with Christ.
- A renewed heart, bearing His image.
- The ability to lead others toward Him — not by force, but by the fragrance of your life.

## Pressing On to the Fullness of Christ

Spiritual maturity a progressive journey unto perfection. It is the ongoing pursuit of Christlikeness, shaped by Scripture, fuelled by prayer, cultivated in community, and expressed through service. It may not be an easy road, but journey is worth it in the end.

And at every stage, from newborn to seasoned saint, we hold to this truth: *We are complete in Him* (Colossians 2:10).

# 8

## COMMUNITY IN CHRIST

Being *complete in Him* is meant to be a shared inheritance between all believers. Salvation may be personal, but sanctification is deeply communal. God never intended for us to grow in isolation. From the very beginning, He placed His people in families, tribes, and churches, because fullness in Christ is discovered most fully *in the Body of Christ*.

The Church of Christ is a living, breathing organism that is diverse in gifting, united in purpose, rooted in love, and held together by Christ Himself. In this chapter, we explore how our completeness in Christ finds its expression in community, and why every believer is both a recipient and a contributor in God's divine family.

# Finding Our Place in God's People

*"For just as the body is one and has many members... so it is with Christ."*
**(1 Corinthians 12:12–13)**

The Church is not a building, a denomination, or a livestream link; it is a spiritual body made up of believers, each one uniquely designed and divinely placed. We are one body with many parts (Romans 12:5). And just as every organ in a human body has a function, so every believer has a God-given role. No one is redundant. No one is accidental. Christ is the head (Colossians 1:18), and we are His hands, His heart, His voice on the earth.

## Responsibilities Within the Body

Belonging to the body comes with blessing and responsibility. It involves:

- *Fellowship:* We commit to walking together, not just attending together (Acts 2:42).

- *Service:* We use our gifts to strengthen others (1 Peter 4:10).

- *Accountability:* We love enough to correct and encourage (Hebrews 10:24–25).

To say "I belong to Christ" is to also say "I belong to His people."

## One Body, Many Gifts

*"Make every effort to keep the unity of the Spirit through the bond of peace."*
**(Ephesians 4:3–4)**

Jesus prayed for oneness in His Church (John 17:21). This prayer was not for uniformity or sameness, but spirit-breathed unity. This unity is not man-made; it is Spirit-preserved. It requires humility, forgiveness, and a shared focus on Christ.

## Diversity by Design

*"There are varieties of gifts, but the same Spirit..."*
**(1 Corinthians 12:4–6)**

The beauty of the Church is not in uniformity but in divine diversity – different callings, cultures, gifts, and graces, including teaching, serving, giving, encouraging, leading, and more (Romans 12:6–8). Each gift is needed. Each part matters (1 Corinthians 12:17–21). And each believer contributes to the collective completeness of the Church.

## Overcoming Division

If division is a disease in the body, then love is the antidote. In order to walk in love, we need to:

- *Avoid comparison* – you are not called to be someone else (Galatians 6:4–5).

- *Embrace differences* – honour all backgrounds and callings (Romans 14:19).

- *Pursue reconciliation* – deal with conflict like Christ (Matthew 18:15–17).

A body divided against itself cannot reflect the wholeness of Christ.

# Building Each Other Up in Love and Truth

*"...to equip the saints for the work of ministry, for building up the body of Christ..."*
**(Ephesians 4:11–12)**

The Church is God's growth environment. It's where teaching sharpens our minds, encouragement lifts our hearts, and accountability strengthens our resolve.

Here are ways we build one another up:

1. *Encouragement:* speaking life daily (Hebrews 3:13).

2. *Teaching and Discipleship:* multiplying maturity (2 Timothy 2:2).

3. *Practical Love:* meeting real needs (Galatians

6:2).

4. *Accountability:* sharpening one another (Proverbs 27:17).

A church that edifies is a church that matures.

## The Bond of Love

> *"A new commandment I give you... love one another: just as I have loved you..."*
> **(John 13:34–35)**

Love is the glue of true community. It binds everything together in perfect harmony (Colossians 3:14). Without it, unity is hollow and service becomes self-serving.

Love looks like:

- Patience when others stumble.

- Kindness when others hurt.

- Selflessness when it's inconvenient (1 Corinthians 13:4–7).

Where love reigns, the Spirit moves freely.

## Living in Community

Being planted brings fruitfulness.
- Don't just attend, engage.

- Don't just receive, serve.

- Don't resist correction, grow from it.

### Meaningful Relationships
Faith flourishes in friendship.
- Invest in **spirit-led relationships**.

- Pursue **mentorship and discipleship**.

- Break barriers; choose reconciliation over resentment.

### Hospitality and Generosity
Genuine community isn't built in pews alone; it's built around tables.
- Open your **home** and your **heart** (Romans 12:13).

- Share your time, your talents, your testimony (Acts 2:45).

Radical hospitality creates a place where God's love becomes visible.

## Conclusion: We Are Complete Together

We are saved individually but completed collectively. The Church is God's chosen vessel for growth, love, correction, and mission. And when we function as one body, we reflect the fullness of Christ on earth. You are an essential part of the Body. Your gifts matter. Your love strengthens others.

In the Church, we discover this timeless truth in full colour: *We are complete in Him and in one another.*

# 9

## MISSION AND PURPOSE

### COMPLETE TO BE COMMISSIONED

To be complete in Christ is not to sit idle in spiritual satisfaction. It is to stand ready – *sent, sealed, and stirred* for mission. From the moment we receive Christ's fullness, we receive His call to go, shine, build, love, and make disciples. He called us to transform the world.

The Christian life is not merely about being saved; it's about *being sent*. Our completeness in Him comes with a divine assignment. We are not trophies on heaven's shelf. We are tools in God's hands, crafted for purpose, carried by grace, and commissioned for impact.

This chapter explores what it means to live on mission, with Jesus at the centre and the world as our field.

# Commissioned by Christ: Stewards of the Great Assignment

*"Go therefore and make disciples of all nations..."*
**(Matthew 28:19)**

Jesus He declared this commission with all authority. The Great Commission is not a suggestion for the spiritual elite; it is the shared call of every believer. Whether your mission field is across the globe or across the street, the command is the same: To go, teach, baptise, and make disciples.

And we are not alone. Jesus said, "You will receive power..." (Acts 1:8). The Spirit empowers where the mission demands.

## What It Means to Be Commissioned

To be commissioned is to be:

- *Called:* You did not choose Him, He chose *you* (John 15:16).

- *Sent:* Commission implies movement, which is faith with feet.

- *Global-minded:* Our gospel is for *every tribe, tongue, and nation.*

Wherever you are, you are on assignment.

## Overcoming the Barriers

Obedience to the Great Commission requires courage, clarity, and commitment.

- *Fear of rejection?* Trust His Spirit to speak through you (Matthew 10:19–20).

- *Lack of knowledge?* Grow through study and mentoring (2 Timothy 2:15).

- *Distractions?* Choose calling over comfort (Luke 9:23).

God doesn't call the equipped; He equips the called.

# Living with Purpose: Walking in God's Plan Daily

*"For we are His workmanship, created in Christ Jesus for good works..."*
**(Ephesians 2:10)**

God's plan for you is deliberate, designed, and already in motion. You were handcrafted for a purpose that carries eternal weight. Not just to exist — but to **impact**. Not just to be busy, but to **bear fruit**.

## Discovering Your Calling

Every believer has a unique role. Some will lead thousands. Others will raise children. Some will preach, others will serve in silence. Each one is vital.

Some of the ways you can discern your purpose include the following:

1. *Pray* – Invite God to reveal His plan (Proverbs 3:5–6).

2. *Know your gifts* – Explore your wiring (1 Corinthians 12:4–6).

3. *Listen to wise counsel* – God often speaks through people (Proverbs 11:14).

4. *Take action* – Faith without works is fantasy (James 2:17).

Purpose isn't something you randomly find; you step into it through activity.

## Purpose in the Everyday

Your mission field is not far; it begins where your feet are.

- In **your family**: Raising the next generation in truth (Deuteronomy 6:6–7).

- In **your workplace**: Working with integrity and witness (Colossians 3:23–24).

- In **your community**: Serving and shining where it's darkest (Matthew 5:14–16).

Purpose isn't limited to the pulpit — it's expressed in the everyday.

## Impacting the World

> *"You are the salt of the earth... the light of the world..."*
> **(Matthew 5:13–14)**

The world doesn't need more noise. It needs light. And it needs salt, truth with flavour, conviction with compassion. You are Christ's ambassador (2 Corinthians 5:20). Where you go, His message goes. His love flows. His glory shows.

## Share Boldly, Live Authentically

The gospel is not just good news; it's the *only* news that saves.

- Share your testimony: your story carries power.

- Live with integrity: your lifestyle speaks louder than sermons.

- Speak the truth in love: people are hungry for authenticity.

The harvest is ripe, and you are the labourer God's been waiting on.

## Discipleship: Multiply the Mission

Jesus commissioned His disciples to "make disciples... teaching them to obey..." (Matthew 28:19–20). So, if evangelism births believers, discipleship grows them.

To disciple is to:

- Teach the Word faithfully.

- Walk with people patiently.

- Model Christ consistently.

Discipleship is not just a curriculum; it is relationship.

## Service and Social Impact

Jesus didn't just preach to souls; He touched lepers, fed crowds, welcomed children.

Likewise, we must **serve holistically**:

- **Meet practical needs** (Matthew 25:35–40).

- **Advocate for justice** with grace and truth.

- **Influence culture** with Kingdom values.

Faith with hands becomes hope in hard places.

## Conclusion: Living Sent and Living Full

To be complete in Christ is not to be static; it is to be **sent**. You were born for this moment. You were saved for this mission. You were filled to be poured out. You are commissioned to spread the gospel. You are called to a divine purpose. You are empowered to impact the world.

As you live on mission, in word, in deed, in love, you reflect the fullness of Christ to a world aching for redemption. And this is the beauty of completeness: it doesn't stop with us. It flows through us.

# 10

## COMPLETE IN CHRIST

### A PERSONAL TESTIMONY

*"For in Him dwells all the fullness of the Godhead bodily; and you are complete in Him..."*
**(Colossians 2:9–10 NKJV)**

This verse changed my life, not as a slogan or a theological phrase, but as a living truth, a truth that walked into the restless corridors of my youth and settled the ache in my soul. If it weren't so, you wouldn't be holding this book in your hands.

## The Search for Love in All the Wrong Places

My battle with incompleteness began early, in the turbulence of adolescence. I searched desperately for love and meaning, but my compass was broken. I wandered into wrong places, clung to wrong relationships, crossed borders and oceans in pursuit of a fulfilment that continually slipped through my fingers.

I was like the song by Foreigner: *"I wanna know what love is... I want you to show me..."* It became my silent anthem, my whispered prayer, and heaven heard it.

## From Longing to Living

Jesus found me in my twenties, and that was the day *life* truly began. Everything changed. My world was unmade and remade.

- From a **hypochondriac**, I became **healthy**.

- From a **lonely soul**, I became **lively**.

- From a **fearful heart**, I became **faith-filled**.

- From **sorrow**, He gave me **song**.

Christ didn't just heal me, He *completed* me.

The impact Christ had in my life wasn't instant, but it was intentional. He gently stripped away the illusions I had latched onto – relationships, approval, image, even finances – and He redirected my desires toward Himself. He raised up disciplers to walk with me. They brought order, correction, and instruction, often with firm love. Today, I'm grateful for every hard lesson.

## The Deep Work of Christ

Jesus became my Friend, Father, Confidant, and Counsellor. Through every trial, every breakthrough, He became more real. And His Word, His precious Word became like food to me. I understand now why Job said:

> *"I have esteemed the words of His mouth*
> *more than my necessary food."*
> **(Job 23:12)**

Years passed, and with every passing season, my only regret became this: *Why didn't I meet Him sooner?* The enemy had painted God as boring, restrictive, and joyless. But I've danced more in Christ than I ever did outside Him. I've laughed more, lived fuller, loved deeper, and found *pleasure without pressure.*

> *"In Your presence is fullness of joy; at Your right hand are pleasures forevermore."*
> **(Psalm 16:11)**

I discovered a truth the world can't sell: *Worldly pleasure offers thrill but brings guilt. Godly pleasure brings peace without regret.*

## A New Kind of Biology

As my journey unfolded, the Lord opened my eyes to see how life in Christ mirrors the very characteristics of living things in biology:

1. *Movement:* In Christ, we *move* with divine purpose. *"In Him we live and move and have our being" (Acts 17:28).*

2. *Respiration:* His breath makes us living souls. We live because He breathes in us. *(Genesis 2:7).*

3. *Nutrition:* We feed on the Word. Without it, our spirit weakens. *"Abide in Me... for apart from Me you can do nothing"* (John 15:4–5).

4. *Irritability:* Outside of Him, like fish out of water, we become restless. But when Christ fills the God-shaped void, true peace reigns.

5. *Growth:* Read your Bible, pray every day..." is still the timeless path. There are no shortcuts or gimmicks, only grace and daily communion.

6. *Excretion:* His Word purifies us. As we digest His truth, the impurities of the flesh are flushed out. *"You are already clean because of the word I have spoken to you"* (John 15:3).

7. *Reproduction:* Every believer is meant to multiply, in soul-winning, in bearing spiritual fruit, in reproducing Christ in others. *"This is to My Father's glory, that you bear much fruit"* (John 15:8).

We are not called to just survive; we are born to **thrive** and **reproduce** for the glory of God.

## A Life Redeemed and Restored

I am grateful that God didn't just save me, He also restored me. He gave me a godly husband, beautiful children, meaningful work, and victory upon victory. Everything the enemy tried to steal, God returned with interest. He crowned my brokenness with joy, adorned my ashes with beauty, and rewrote my sorrow with songs of deliverance. And yet, it is *not the blessings* that complete me. It is *Christ alone*. He is the Source, the Centre, the Shepherd of my soul. "He is a jealous God," not because He is insecure, but because He alone knows that nothing else will ever satisfy.

## Freedom Through the Word

There were specific Scriptures that broke chains in my life. For instance:

- **Fear of death** was shattered by Hebrews 2:14–15: *"He shared in our humanity... to free those who all their lives were held in slavery by their fear of death."*

- **Worry** dissolved through Matthew 6:25–34:

> *"Do not worry about your life... your Father knows what you need."*

Over and over, the Word cut through the lies like a sword.

## A Final Word – And a Prayer

Time would fail me to recount every victory, every miracle, every whisper from the Holy Spirit. But here's what I know: I am no longer searching.
I have found what I was made for. *I am complete in Him.*

And so are you.

## A Simple Prayer for Completeness

If you've read this far, I believe it's for a reason. Will you pray with me?

*Dear Heavenly Father,*
*I want to know and experience You like never before.*
*Come into my life afresh. Rearrange me.*
*Take control of my entire being.*
*Make me complete in You, and may I never look elsewhere for what only You can give.*

*Lead me to spend eternity with You, beginning now.*
*Order my steps, O Lord, until I see You face to face.*
*In Jesus' name, Amen.*

Now rise, dear reader, and go live as one who is truly, gloriously, *completely complete* in Christ. You are loved. You are called. You are complete.

## Conclusion

### Walking in the Fullness of Christ

To be complete in Christ is not simply a truth to believe; it's a life to be lived. It means waking each day with the assurance that we lack nothing in Him, and stepping into a world in need with hearts full of grace, purpose, and boldness. Let this not be the end of a book, but the beginning of a deeper walk. Keep seeking. Keep growing. Keep walking in the truth that *you are complete in Him* – today, tomorrow, and forever.

# Appendices

## 1. Study Questions: For Personal Reflection or Group Discussion

These questions can help you process the themes of this book, either on your own or in a group setting.

1. What does it mean to be complete in Christ? How does this truth challenge your personal understanding of identity?

2. What are some areas where you still struggle to see Christ as sufficient?

3. How does understanding Christ's deity strengthen your faith?

4. What role has the Holy Spirit played in your journey toward spiritual maturity?

5. How does your view of completeness affect

how you approach relationships and community?

6. What steps can you take to actively live out your mission and purpose in Christ?

7. How can you bring Christ's completeness to others in your workplace, home, or church?

8. What spiritual disciplines can you implement to stay rooted in Christ daily?

## 2. Further Reading: Recommended Books and Resources

For those who want to dive deeper into the themes explored in this book, here are some recommended resources:

- *Knowing God* – J.I. Packer
- *The Pursuit of God* – A.W. Tozer
- *Victory in Christ* – Charles Trumbull
- *The Spirit-Filled Life* – Charles Stanley
- *Discipleship Essentials* – Greg Ogden

## 3. Scripture References: Key Verses on Completeness in Christ

Here are some key passages that reinforce the message of this book:

- **Colossians 2:9-10** – "For in Him the whole fullness of deity dwells bodily, and you have been filled in Him."

- **John 15:5** – "Apart from Me, you can do nothing."

- **Ephesians 1:3** – "Blessed be the God and Father of our Lord Jesus Christ, who has blessed us in Christ with every spiritual blessing."

- **2 Corinthians 5:17** – "If anyone is in Christ, he is a new creation."

- **Romans 8:37** – "In all these things we are more than conquerors through Him who loved us."

- **Philippians 4:13** – "I can do all things through Christ who strengthens me."

www.ingramcontent.com/pod-product-compliance
Lightning Source LLC
Chambersburg PA
CBHW061453040426
42450CB00007B/1342